FATHERING STRONG

The Father You Were Made To Be

Playbook

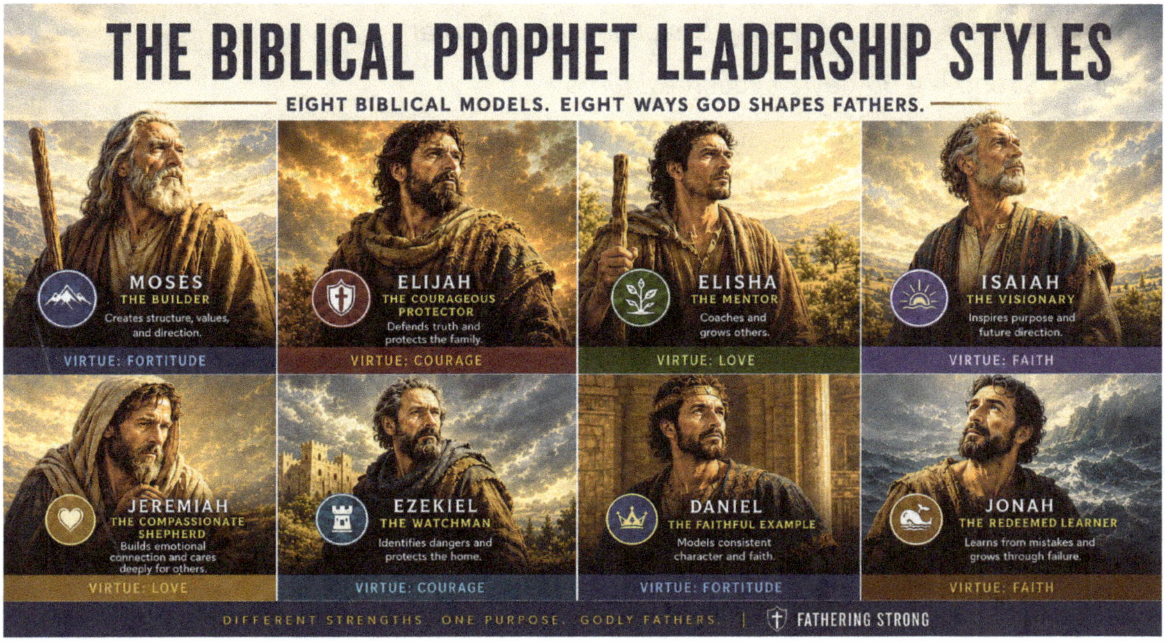

Discover the Leadership Style God Has Developed in You

BRUCE STAPLETON

MOVEMENTUM PRESS

Published by Movementum Press

www.movementum.com

All rights reserved. No part of this book may be used or reproduced by any means, graphic, electronic, or mechanical, including photocopying, recording, taping, or by any information storage retrieval system without the written permission of the author except in the case of brief quotations embodied in critical articles and reviews.

This book is a work of non-fiction. Unless otherwise noted, the author and the publisher make no explicit guarantees as to the accuracy of the information in this book.

This book is a part of the Fathering Strong Fatherhood Series of publications and may be ordered by going to www.fatheringstrongbook.com.

Other resources authored by Bruce Stapleton referenced in this book include:

Fathering Strong – God's Blueprint for Leading Your Family

Fatherhood Awakening and 30-day Devotional and Journal

Fathering Strong – A 90-day Devotional Journey

Because of the dynamic nature of the Internet, any web addresses or links contained in this book may have changed since publication and may no longer be valid.

Scripture quotations are taken from the Holy Bible, NEW INTERNATIONAL VERSION, NIV Copyright© 1973, 1978, 1984, 2011 by Biblica, Inc. Used by permission. All rights reserved worldwide.

Scripture quotations are from the ESV® Bible (The Holy Bible, English Standard Version®), copyright© 2001 by Crossway Bibles, a publishing ministry of Good News Publishers. Used by permission. All rights reserved.

ISBN: 978-1-972132-04-3

Copyright © 2026 Bruce Stapleton

Table of Contents

Why I Wrote This Playbook

I didn't set out to write a book about leadership styles. I set out to become a better father.

The first time I held my newborn daughter, her tiny fingers wrapped around mine, I felt overwhelmed with happiness, wonder, and an immense sense of responsibility. I promised myself I would be the best father I could be. Like many new fathers, I stood there both excited and uncertain about the journey ahead.

That uncertainty didn't go away. I remember sitting in my car after a particularly rough day, my son's angry voice still ringing in my ears from our latest argument, wondering how I'd gotten it so wrong.

Looking back now, one of my biggest regrets is not understanding sooner just how crucial it is to build deep, intentional relationships with your children. I spent so many years caught up in being the provider — making sure there was food on the table and the bills were paid — that I missed precious moments to simply connect with my kids while they were young.

If I could go back and do it all over, I would have approached fatherhood differently from day one. I would have wanted a mirror — something to show me, clearly and without judgment, the kind of leader I already was becoming, and the kind God was still shaping me into.

That's what sent me back to Scripture, looking not for another list of parenting rules, but for real men — Moses, Elijah, Jonah, and the rest — who led imperfectly and were used by God anyway. What I found is that God never used one template to build a father. He used builders and protectors, mentors and watchmen, visionaries and shepherds — men with real strengths and real failures, who were faithful with what they had been given.

This playbook is the tool I wish I'd had years ago. My prayer is that it helps you see, clearly and without shame, the father God has already begun shaping in you — and the next step He is calling you to take.

— *Bruce Stapleton*

How to Use Your Playbook

This playbook is designed for personal reflection, not passive reading. Each chapter introduces one of eight Prophetic Fatherhood Leadership Styles drawn from Scripture, and invites you to apply what you learn directly to your own life as a father.

What You'll Find in Each Chapter

- **Scripture** — The biblical foundation for each leadership style.
- **Apply This to My Life** — Prompts that shift the content from information to personal application.
- **Strengths and Blind Spots** — Honest self-assessment tools.
- **Personal Reflection** — Journaling questions with space to write.
- **My Action Plan** — Concrete next steps you commit to before moving on.

Getting the Most Out of Your Playbook

Go slow. This is not a book to race through. Spend a week—or longer—on each leadership style. Let the questions do their work.

Write honestly. These pages are for you. No one is grading your answers. The more honest you are, the more useful this process will be.

Pray through it. Before each chapter, ask God to show you what He wants you to see about your fathering.

Revisit it. Come back to this playbook in six months or a year. Growth is not a one-time event.

Who This Playbook Is For

This playbook was written with fathers in mind — but fatherhood takes more shapes than one. If you are a biological dad, adoptive or foster father, stepfather, single father, or a grandfather raising grandchildren, the eight leadership styles in this playbook apply to you. So does the invitation: to lead the children in your care with structure, courage, mentorship, vision, compassion, discernment, integrity, and humility.

If you are walking through fatherhood without a partner, a few of the reflection questions assume a two-parent household. Adapt the wording as you go — the virtue underneath each question still applies.

This playbook also works well as a shared resource. Many fathers go through it alongside a men's group, small group at church, or even with a teenage or adult child, using one chapter's reflection questions as discussion prompts rather than private journaling alone.

Why These Eight Prophets?

The eight prophets in this playbook were not chosen because they were perfect men. They were chosen because each of them embodied a distinct kind of leadership that God used to serve, protect, build, and transform the people around them—and because every one of those leadership qualities is needed in the home.

Together, they give us a complete picture of what strong, God-dependent fatherhood looks like. And taken individually, each one speaks directly to a type of father who is present in every generation—including yours.

Moses—The Builder

Moses was chosen because he built something from nothing. Leading a nation of former slaves through the wilderness, he created systems, established values, and kept people moving toward a destination they could not yet see. He is the model for every father who understands that his family needs more than provision—it needs structure, direction, and a vision for where it is going.

Elijah—The Courageous Protector

Elijah was chosen because he refused to compromise when every cultural pressure said to do exactly that. Standing alone against the prophets of Baal, confronting a corrupt king, calling out what was false in the name of what was true—Elijah models the father who understands that protection is not just physical. It is spiritual. It is moral. It is the courage to say "not in this house" when the world says otherwise.

Elisha—The Mentor

Elisha was chosen because his entire ministry was defined by investment in others. He followed Elijah faithfully, received the mantle, and then poured himself into the people around him. Elisha is the model for fathers who know that their greatest legacy is not what they accomplish but what they develop in others—particularly in their own children.

Isaiah—The Visionary

Isaiah was chosen because he could see what was coming when no one else could. In the darkest seasons of Israel's history, he spoke of restoration, purpose, and a future that only God could bring about. Fathers who carry a sense of God's purpose for their family—who speak vision over their children and keep hope alive in their home—reflect Isaiah's gift.

Jeremiah—The Compassionate Shepherd

Jeremiah was chosen because he stayed. He is sometimes called the weeping prophet, and that description reveals his greatest strength: he felt the weight of what his people were carrying and he did not look away. He wept. He pleaded. He remained emotionally present in a culture that rejected his message. Fathers who lead through empathy and relational depth—who move toward their family in pain rather than away from it—walk in Jeremiah's footsteps.

Ezekiel—The Watchman

Ezekiel was chosen because God specifically appointed him as a watchman—someone stationed at the wall to identify danger before it arrived and to warn the people in time. The Watchman father sees what others miss. He pays attention to the spiritual and cultural currents affecting his family. He does not wait for damage to occur before he acts. He is alert, discerning, and responsible.

Daniel—The Faithful Example

Daniel was chosen because his faithfulness was quiet, consistent, and unbreakable. Taken into captivity as a young man, he spent his entire life serving pagan rulers without compromising his identity or his God. He never had the platform of a Moses or the boldness of an Elijah—but the people around him saw something different in him and could not deny it. Fathers who lead through integrity and consistent character, day after day and year after year, are Daniel's kind of father.

Jonah—The Redeemed Learner

Jonah was chosen precisely because he ran. He resisted his calling, failed spectacularly, hit rock bottom in the most dramatic way imaginable—and was restored. And from that restoration, he went on to see one of the greatest awakenings in the Old Testament. Jonah is included not in spite of his failures but because of what God did through them. He is the model for every father who has made serious mistakes and wonders whether God can still use him.

Eight Prophets. Many Flaws. One God.

It would be easy to look at this list of prophets and assume that God chose them because they were exceptional men—men who had it all together, who never doubted, never failed, and never let anyone down. The opposite is true.

Moses lost his temper and struck the rock when God told him to speak to it—and it cost him the Promised Land. Elijah, the same prophet who called down fire from heaven, collapsed under a tree and begged God to let him die. Jeremiah wanted to quit. Isaiah declared himself hopelessly unworthy the moment he stood in the presence of God. Jonah actively ran in the opposite direction from where God was sending him. Daniel spent his life as a captive in a foreign land, serving men who did not know his God.

And yet God used every one of them. Not despite their flaws, but through a relationship with them that was honest about those flaws and committed to something greater.

Every father carries the same reality. There are areas where you are naturally strong—where leadership comes easily, where your family benefits from what God has placed in you. And there are areas where you struggle, where you fall short, where the gap between who you want to be and who you are feels wide.

The challenge of fatherhood is not to become someone you are not. It is to steward what you are. To lean into your God-given strengths with intention and humility. To acknowledge your weaknesses honestly and invite God to work in them rather than hiding them from your family.

These eight prophets give you a language for that process. They show you what it looks like when God takes a man with a distinct set of gifts—and limitations—and uses him to build something that lasts. A nation. A movement. A revival. A legacy.

In your case: a family.

The Four Virtues of Fathering Strong

Every leadership style in this playbook is anchored to one of four core virtues: Courage, Fortitude, Faith, and Love. These are not abstract ideals. They are active, living qualities that define how strong fathers lead their families every day. Understanding these virtues—and recognizing where you are strong and where you need to grow—is the foundation of everything that follows.

As explored in depth in Fathering Strong: God's Blueprint for Leading Your Family (Stapleton, 2025), these four virtues work together as a unified framework. Courage enables you to act. Fortitude keeps you standing. Faith gives you direction. And love fuels them all.

Courage — Facing the World Head-On

> *"For though the righteous fall seven times, they rise again."* — **Proverbs 24:16**

Courage is the virtue that enables you to act on everything else you believe. While faith gives direction, fortitude provides endurance, and love fuels purpose, it is courage that transforms those qualities from ideals into action. Courage is not the absence of fear—it is choosing to move forward despite fear, driven by love for your children and dedication to your family.

Fatherhood demands courage in ways that rarely look heroic from the outside: the courage to set boundaries your children resist, to admit when you have been wrong, to protect your family from harmful influences, to step into uncertainty without knowing how things will turn out, and to be emotionally present even when vulnerability feels risky. Every day, faithful fathers face tough choices and must grow in areas where they feel inadequate. Courage is what makes that growth possible.

Fortitude — The Unwavering Strength of a Father's Heart

> *"Be strong and courageous. Do not be afraid; do not be discouraged, for the Lord your God will be with you wherever you go."* — **Joshua 1:9**

Fatherhood is not a sprint; it is a marathon. Fortitude is the inner strength that keeps you in the race long after the initial energy of good intentions has faded. It is what helps you persevere through adversity—through the 3 AM feedings, through the teenage rebellions, through job loss and health crises and seasons when everything seems to be going wrong at once.

Fortitude is not about being unaffected by hardship. It is about moving forward despite it. Like a tree that develops deeper roots in response to strong winds, the father who perseveres through difficulty grows stronger through it—not just for himself, but for those who depend on him. Scripture's model for this is not a man who never struggles; it is a man like Job, who declared even in his suffering, "Though he slay me, yet will I hope in him" (Job 13:15). Fortitude is spiritual endurance as much as it is emotional resolve.

Faith — The Anchoring Strength of a Fathering Strong Life

> *"Faith gives us the wisdom to know when to stand firm, courage provides the strength to face our fears, fortitude helps us persevere through challenges, and love guides our every action."* — **Fathering Strong**

Faith is not simply a personal belief system—it is a transformative force that shapes every dimension of fatherhood. It serves as a moral compass in ethical decisions, a source of hope and resilience in hardship, a foundation for inner strength during life's toughest battles, and a framework for raising children who understand they are part of something larger than themselves.

For fathers, faith means trusting that God is working even when outcomes are invisible. It means leading your family through seasons of uncertainty not with false confidence, but with genuine trust in divine provision. Faith does not make the path easier—but combined with courage, fortitude, and love, it creates an unshakeable foundation. It reminds you that you are not alone in the sacred work of raising your children.

Love — The Heart of Fathering Strong

> *"Do everything in love." — 1 Corinthians 16:14*

Love is not simply one of the four virtues—it is the driving force behind all of them. Courage without love becomes aggression. Fortitude without love becomes stubbornness. Faith without love becomes rigidity. But love transforms all of these qualities into something that actually reaches a child's heart.

A father can provide material comforts and set wise boundaries, but those actions feel mechanical without love as their foundation. Love turns discipline into guidance, and everyday moments into lasting memories. As Scripture declares, *"Perfect love drives out fear"* (1 John 4:18)—and *"rooted and established in love"* (Ephesians 3:17-19), you are equipped to do more than you ever imagined as a father. Love shows up. Even when it is inconvenient, exhausting, or costly—**love shows up.**

How the Virtues Connect to the Leadership Styles

Each leadership style in this playbook embodies one or more of these four virtues.

COURAGE Elijah (Courageous Protector) · Ezekiel (Watchman)
FORTITUDE Moses (Builder) · Daniel (Faithful Example)
FAITH Isaiah (Visionary) · Jonah (Redeemed Learner)
LOVE Elisha (Mentor) · Jeremiah (Compassionate Shepherd)

As you work through each chapter, notice which virtue feels most natural to you and which one is calling you to grow.

For Further Reading: Chapters 3—6 of *Fathering Strong: God's Blueprint for Leading Your Family* by Bruce Stapleton explore each of these four virtues in depth through real stories, biblical wisdom, and practical application. Available at **www.fatheringstrongbook.com**.

The Eight Leadership Styles

1. Moses — The Builder (Core Virtue: Fortitude)
2. Elijah — The Courageous Protector (Core Virtue: Courage)
3. Elisha — The Mentor (Core Virtue: Love)
4. Isaiah — The Visionary (Core Virtue: Faith)
5. Jeremiah — The Compassionate Shepherd (Core Virtue: Love)
6. Ezekiel — The Watchman (Core Virtue: Courage)
7. Daniel — The Faithful Example (Core Virtue: Fortitude)
8. Jonah — The Redeemed Learner (Core Virtue: Faith)

Before you begin, answer this question:

What kind of father do I most want to become, and what is one thing currently holding me back?

The Fatherhood Leadership Style Assessment

Complete this assessment before engaging with the chapters. Rate how each statement describes you as you currently are—not as you aspire to be. There are no right or wrong answers. Your results will guide your self-reflection and growth throughout this playbook.

You can also take this assessment online at https://fatheringstrongbook.com/archetype/ or scan the QR code.

Rating Scale

1 = Strongly Disagree
2 = Disagree
3 = Neutral
4 = Agree
5 = Strongly Agree

SECTION 1 OF 8

The Builder (Moses)

Virtue: Fortitude | Core Strength: Responsibility

Statement	1	2	3	4	5	Score
1. I naturally create plans and systems.						___
2. My family looks to me for direction.						___
3. I think about long-term family goals.						___
4. I enjoy establishing routines and structure.						___
5. I feel responsible for creating stability.						___

Total Score (out of 25): ______ / 25

SECTION 2 OF 8

The Courageous Protector (Elijah)

Virtue: Courage | Core Strength: Courage

Statement	1	2	3	4	5	Score
6. I willingly confront difficult issues.						___
7. I speak up when something is wrong.						___
8. I prioritize protecting my family from harmful influences.						___
9. I am willing to stand alone for what is right.						___
10. I remain calm during crises.						___

Total Score (out of 25): ______ / 25

SECTION 3 OF 8

The Mentor (Elisha)

Virtue: Love | Core Strength: Development

Statement	1	2	3	4	5	Score
11. I enjoy teaching and coaching others.						___
12. I look for opportunities to encourage growth.						___
13. I am patient when helping others learn.						___
14. I celebrate the success of those I mentor.						___
15. I intentionally invest in younger people.						___

Total Score (out of 25): _____ / 25

SECTION 4 OF 8

The Visionary (Isaiah)

Virtue: Faith | Core Strength: Vision

Statement	1	2	3	4	5	Score
16. I often think about the future.						___
17. I enjoy helping others see possibilities.						___
18. I communicate purpose and direction.						___
19. I naturally inspire others.						___
20. I focus on what could become rather than what currently exists.						___

Total Score (out of 25): _____ / 25

SECTION 5 OF 8

The Compassionate Shepherd (Jeremiah)

Virtue: Love | Core Strength: Empathy

Statement	1	2	3	4	5	Score
21. People often share personal struggles with me.						___
22. I am comfortable discussing emotions.						___
23. I listen carefully before offering advice.						___
24. I feel deeply connected to those I love.						___
25. I notice when family members are hurting.						___

Total Score (out of 25): _____ / 25

SECTION 6 OF 8

The Watchman (Ezekiel)

Virtue: Courage | Core Strength: Discernment

Statement	1	2	3	4	5	Score
26. I quickly recognize potential dangers.						___
27. I pay attention to cultural influences affecting my family.						___
28. I am naturally observant.						___
29. I think proactively about risks.						___
30. I feel responsible for protecting my family spiritually.						___
Total Score (out of 25):						_____ / 25

SECTION 7 OF 8

The Faithful Example (Daniel)

Virtue: Fortitude | Core Strength: Integrity

Statement	1	2	3	4	5	Score
31. I strive to live consistently with my beliefs.						___
32. My actions match my words.						___
33. Others would describe me as dependable.						___
34. I maintain my values even under pressure.						___
35. I prioritize integrity over popularity.						___
Total Score (out of 25):						_____ / 25

SECTION 8 OF 8

The Redeemed Learner (Jonah)

Virtue: Faith | Core Strength: Humility

Statement	1	2	3	4	5	Score
36. I am willing to admit mistakes.						___
37. Failure often becomes a valuable teacher for me.						___
38. I can laugh at my own shortcomings.						___
39. I am continually growing as a father.						___
40. I believe God can use imperfect people.						___
Total Score (out of 25):						_____ / 25

Scoring and Interpretation

Total each section's five questions to get a score out of 25.

Score Ranges		
5—10 =	Emerging	This style is not a current strength—but may be a growth area.
11—17 =	Developing	You show some characteristics of this style; room to grow.
18—22 =	Established	This is a consistent strength in your fatherhood.
23—25 =	Dominant	This is likely your Primary or Secondary Leadership Style.

What Your Results Reveal

Your results do not identify a single "type." Instead, they reveal the combination of leadership strengths that most influence your fatherhood.

Highest Score = Your Primary Leadership Style (the style you most naturally express)
Second Highest = Your Secondary Leadership Style (your supporting strength)
Lowest Score(s) = Your Growth Opportunity (areas God may be developing in you)

My Assessment Summary

Record your scores below and rank them from highest to lowest.

Leadership Style	Virtue	My Score
The Builder (Moses)	Fortitude	_____ /25
The Courageous Protector (Elijah)	Courage	_____ /25
The Mentor (Elisha)	Love	_____ /25
The Visionary (Isaiah)	Faith	_____ /25
The Compassionate Shepherd (Jeremiah)	Love	_____ /25
The Watchman (Ezekiel)	Courage	_____ /25
The Faithful Example (Daniel)	Fortitude	_____ /25
The Redeemed Learner (Jonah)	Faith	_____ /25

My Primary Leadership Style:

____

My Secondary Leadership Style:

____

My Greatest Growth Area:

____

One insight from my results:

Visualize Your Results

Numbers are easy to skim past. A picture is harder to ignore. Using the radar chart below, place a dot on each spoke to match your eight scores from the Assessment Summary on the previous page, then connect the eight dots into one shape. When you are done, you will see your full leadership profile at a glance.

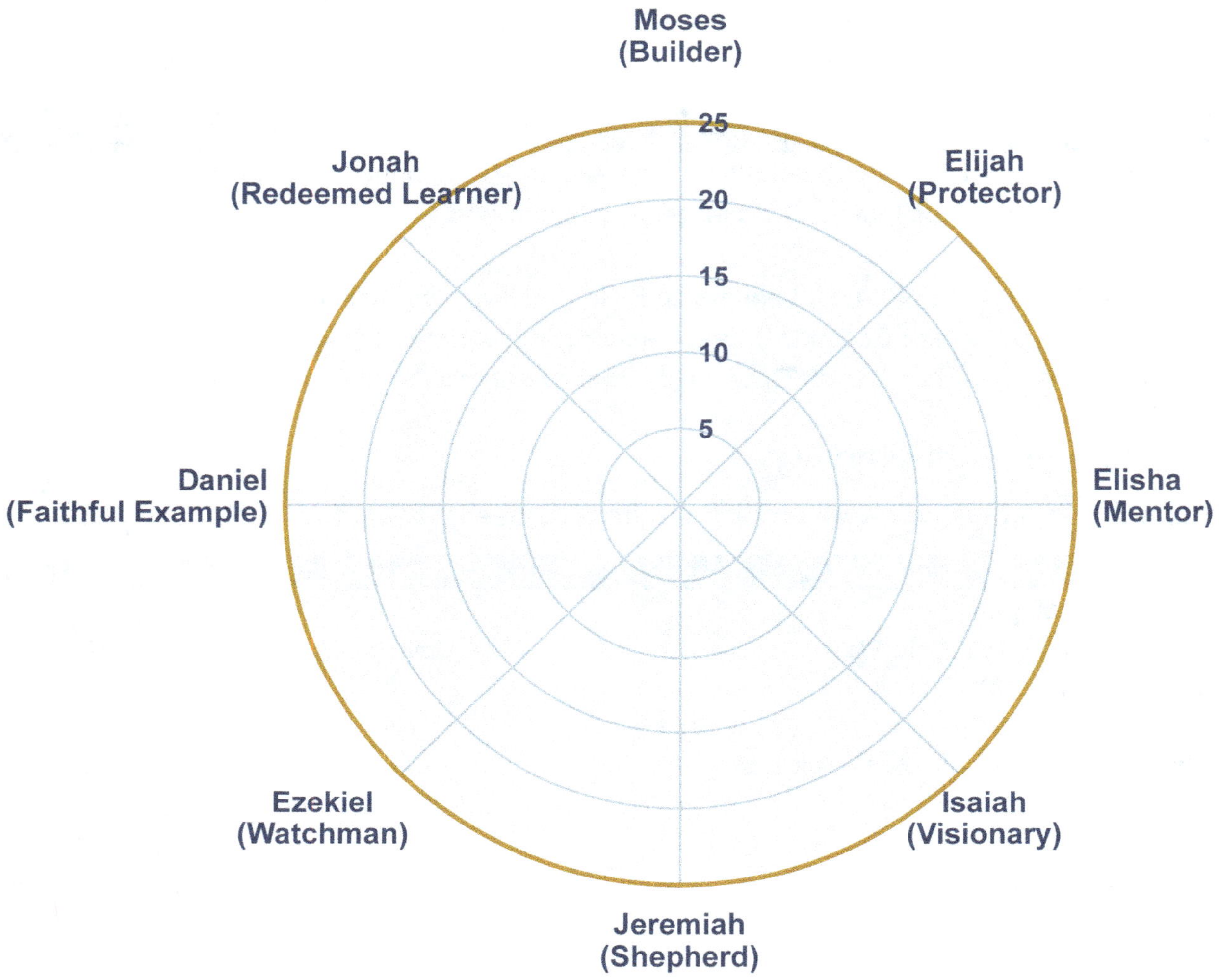

Optional: circle your Primary and Secondary Leadership Style labels once plotted, and mark your lowest score — that is your current Growth Opportunity.

Using Your Results as You Work Through This Playbook

Your assessment results are not a label—they are a lens. Use them to read each chapter with greater awareness, curiosity, and intention.

Your Primary Leadership Style: Lean Into Your Strength

When you reach the chapter that matches your Primary Leadership Style, expect it to feel familiar. You likely already exhibit many of these qualities. The goal here is not discovery, but depth. Go beneath the surface. Ask yourself: How well am I stewarding this gift? Where has this strength produced fruit in my family? Where might it have become an obstacle?

Your Secondary Leadership Style: Recognize Your Range

Your secondary style is the supporting strength that complements your primary. It may show up in different contexts—perhaps at work, in community, or during particular seasons of fatherhood. Use that chapter to explore how this style adds dimension to the way you lead your family.

Your Growth Areas: Embrace the Challenge

The leadership styles where you scored lowest are not weaknesses to be ashamed of. They are areas where God may be inviting you to grow. As you work through those chapters, resist the urge to skip over them. The reflection questions and action steps there will stretch you in ways the others may not.

A Practical Approach

You can work through this playbook in any order, but we recommend starting with your Primary Leadership Style chapter to build confidence, then moving through the others. Return to your Assessment Summary page after each chapter to note any shifts in how you see yourself.

Before You Begin Each Chapter

Look at your Assessment Summary page and ask:

Is this my primary, secondary, or a growth-area leadership style?

What does that tell me about how I should approach this chapter?

What am I most likely to discover here that I might not expect?

Quick Reference Guide: The Eight Leadership Styles at a Glance

Eight biblical prophets, eight fatherhood leadership styles. Use this page as your at-aglance guide before you begin — and flip back to it any time you want a quick reminder of the full framework.

Leadership Style	Virtue	Core Strength	Signature Strenth	Watch For	Key Verse
Moses - The Builder	Fortitude	Responsibility	Creates stability & structure	Becoming overly controlling	Exodus 18:21
Elijah — The Courageous Protector	Courage	Courage	Confronts issues, protects values	Confusing conviction with harshness	1 Kings 18:21
Elisha — The Mentor	Love	Development	Teaches and develops others	Avoiding necessary discipline	2 Kings 2:9
Isaiah — The Visionary	Faith	Vision	Casts hope-filled vision	Overlooking practical details	Isaiah 40:31
Jeremiah — The Compassionate Shepherd	Love	Empathy	Listens, creates emotional safety	Avoiding necessary correction	Jeremiah 29:11
Ezekiel — The Watchman	Courage	Vigilance	Alert to danger, sets boundaries	Turning protection into control	Ezekiel 3:17
Daniel — The Faithful Example	Fortitude	Integrity	Consistent character under pressure	Being perceived as rigid	Daniel 6:4
Jonah — The Redeemed Learner	Faith	Humility Creates stability & structure	Learns and grows through failure	Avoiding difficult responsibilities	Jonah 3:1

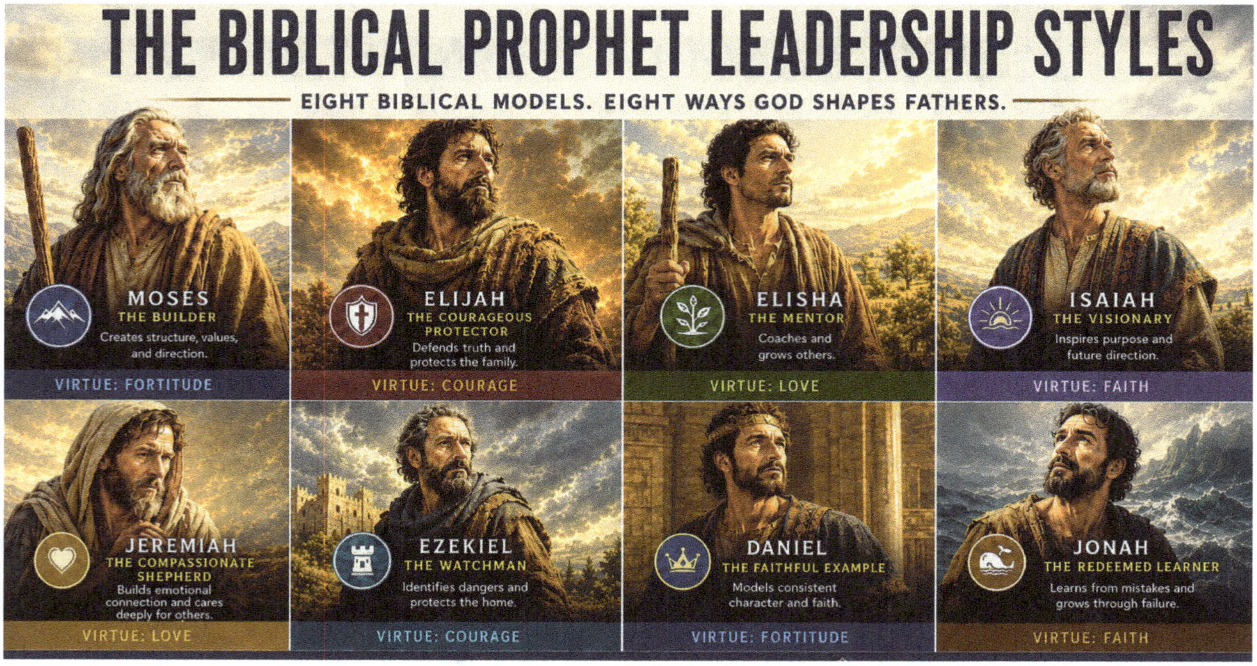

Chapter 1:Moses — The Builder

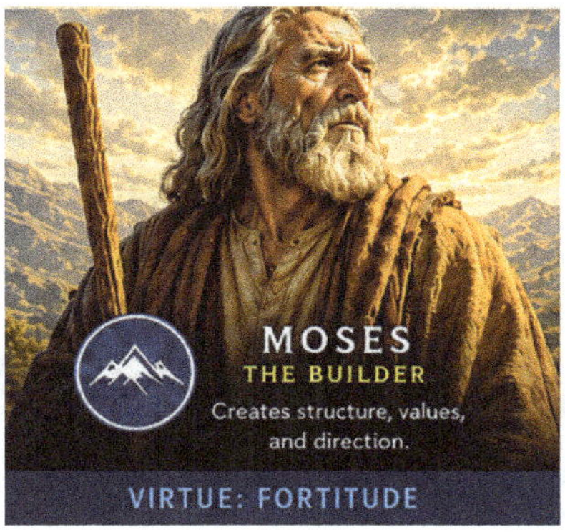

Moses is one of Scripture's most powerful models of fatherhood because his calling was not simply to lead people out of Egypt—it was to build an entire nation. He created structure, established values, and provided direction for generations to come. As you work through this chapter, consider how the Builder leadership style shows up in your own fathering

.

Core Strength: Responsibility

Moses consistently accepted responsibility for people, even when it was difficult.

Scripture: "But Moses sought the favor of the Lord his God." — Exodus 32:11

When Israel rebelled with the golden calf, Moses didn't abandon them. He interceded for them and continued leading.

How Moses Created Structure

> *"Select capable men from all the people—and appoint them as officials over thousands, hundreds, fifties and tens."* — **Exodus 18:21**

Moses was overwhelmed trying to solve every problem himself. His father-in-law Jethro advised him to create leadership structures. Builders understand that healthy systems create stability.

Apply This To My Life

What systems or routines do I currently have in place that help my family thrive?

Where does our family lack structure, and what is one thing I could put in place this week?

How Moses Established Values

> *"These commandments that I give you today are to be on your hearts."* — **Deuteronomy 6:6**

Moses gave Israel a moral framework. Builder fathers intentionally define family values.

Apply This To My Life

What are the top 3 values I am intentionally teaching my children?

How would my children describe our family's values if asked today?

How Moses Provided Direction

> *"The Lord your God is bringing you into a good land."* — **Deuteronomy 8:7**

Even during years of wandering, Moses reminded people where they were headed. Builder fathers create vision. They ask "Where are we going as a family?" rather than merely "How do we get through this week?"

Apply This To My Life

What is the long-term vision I have for my family? Write it out here:

How Moses Built Future Generations

> *"Commission Joshua, and encourage and strengthen him."* — **Deuteronomy 3:28**

Before his death, Moses intentionally prepared Joshua to lead. Builder fathers don't simply raise children—they prepare future husbands, wives, mothers, fathers, and followers of Christ.

Apply This To My Life

In what ways am I intentionally preparing my children for adulthood and leadership?

GO DEEPER

To explore Fortitude in greater depth — including how to build lasting structure without becoming controlling — turn to the Chapter 4: Fortitude chapter in Fathering Strong: God's Blueprint for Leading Your Family.

A BUILDER IN REAL LIFE

Mark didn't think of himself as a "visionary" kind of dad — he just liked things to work. He built one routine: Sunday-night phones off the table, one question for each kid about their week, prayer before bed. It felt small. Three years later, his oldest told him it was the one part of the week she never wanted to miss. Builders rarely see the impact of structure in the moment. They see it years later, in what their kids choose to keep.

Strengths of the Builder Father

- ✔ Creates stability
- ✔ Plans ahead and takes responsibility
- ✔ Protects family values and provides direction
- ✔ Remains dependable during challenges
- ✔ Thinks long-term and generationally

Blind Spots to Watch

- ⚠ Becoming overly controlling
- ⚠ Focusing more on tasks than relationships
- ⚠ Carrying too much responsibility alone
- ⚠ Becoming frustrated when others don't follow the plan
- ⚠ Neglecting emotional connection

Moses needed Aaron, Miriam, Jethro, and Joshua. Builders need support too.

Personal Reflection

What systems have I created that help my family thrive?

Can my family clearly describe our direction and values?

Am I building for the next generation, or simply managing today?

Do my children experience me as a guide, not just a rule-maker?

My Action Plan: The Builder

Based on what you've read, write one specific action you will take this week in each area:

One way I will apply this leadership style in my relationship with my children:

One conversation I need to have:

One habit or pattern I want to strengthen:

I will know I'm growing in this area when—

Fathering Strong Virtue: Fortitude — the strength to remain steady under pressure and build for the long term

Signed: ______________________________ *Date:* ___________

Chapter 2: Elijah — The Courageous Protector

Elijah stands as one of Scripture's clearest examples of moral courage. He lived during a time when Israel had largely abandoned God under the influence of King Ahab and Queen Jezebel. While others remained silent, Elijah confronted falsehood, challenged corruption, and called people back to God's truth. For fathers, Elijah represents the man who is willing to stand firm when it would be easier to compromise.

Core Strength: Courage

Fatherhood Focus: Defending truth and protecting the family from harmful influences.

How Elijah Refused Cultural Compromise

> *"How long will you waver between two opinions? If the Lord is God, follow him; but if Baal is God, follow him."* — **1 Kings 18:21**

On Mount Carmel, Elijah confronted 450 prophets of Baal and challenged the nation to choose. Protectors recognize that not every cultural trend is healthy.

Apply This To My Life

What values or influences are currently shaping my children that I need to address?

Where am I tempted to stay silent when I should speak up?

How Elijah Confronted Powerful People

> *"Have you not murdered a man and seized his property?" — 1 Kings 21:19*

Elijah boldly confronted King Ahab. Protectors speak truth even when it is uncomfortable. Peace is not the absence of conflict—peace is the presence of truth.

Apply This To My Life

What difficult conversation have I been avoiding that needs to happen?

How Elijah Protected Future Generations

"The people fell prostrate and cried, "The Lord—he is God!"" **— 1 Kings 18:39**

When Elijah challenged Baal worship, he wasn't merely fighting a theological battle. He was protecting the next generation. A father protects more than physical safety—he protects beliefs, character, identity, and spiritual health.

Apply This To My Life

What spiritual practices am I modeling that protect my children's faith?

How Elijah Acted During Crisis

"The jar of flour was not used up and the jug of oil did not run dry." **— 1 Kings 17:16**

While others panicked, Elijah remained faithful. Protectors remain steady during uncertainty. Children often look first to their father when life becomes uncertain.

Apply This To My Life

How do I currently lead my family during seasons of hardship or uncertainty?

How Elijah Modeled Faith Under Pressure

"Answer me, Lord, answer me, so these people will know that you, Lord, are God." **— 1 Kings 18:37**

Before God ever sent fire from heaven, Elijah publicly trusted God before seeing the outcome. He risked failure because he trusted God's faithfulness.

Apply This To My Life

What does it look like for me to model faith when circumstances are difficult?

Note: After Mount Carmel, Elijah became exhausted and discouraged. God responded not with criticism but with rest, food, and encouragement. Even protectors need support.

GO DEEPER

To go deeper on Courage — including what it costs to stand alone for what's right, and how to recover when courage leaves you exhausted — turn to the Courage chapter in Fathering Strong: God's Blueprint for Leading Your Family.

A PROTECTOR IN REAL LIFE

When David found troubling content on his 14-year-old's tablet, his first instinct was to avoid the conversation altogether. Instead, he sat down with his son that night, named what he'd found without shame or rage, and stayed in the room until the silence broke. It was an uncomfortable hour. It was also the night his son started actually talking to him. Courageous Protectors don't avoid hard rooms — they walk in and stay.

Strengths of the Courageous Protector Father

- ✔ Confronts problems directly
- ✔ Protects family values and speaks truth with conviction
- ✔ Remains calm during crises
- ✔ Refuses to compromise core beliefs

Blind Spots to Watch

- ⚠ Becoming overly confrontational
- ⚠ Confusing conviction with harshness
- ⚠ Carrying burdens alone
- ⚠ Neglecting emotional connection
- ⚠ Experiencing burnout after prolonged battles

Personal Reflection

What influences am I allowing into my home?

Do my children see me standing for truth in everyday situations?

Am I protecting only physical safety, or also spiritual health?

How can I model courageous faith this week?

My Action Plan: The Courageous Protector

Based on what you've read, write one specific action you will take this week in each area:

One way I will apply this leadership style in my relationship with my children:

One conversation I need to have:

One habit or pattern I want to strengthen:

I will know I'm growing in this area when—

Fathering Strong Virtue: Courage — the willingness to confront danger, stand for truth, and guard what matters most

Signed: ______________________________ *Date:* ____________

Chapter 3: Elisha — The Mentor

While Elijah is remembered for dramatic displays of courage, Elisha is remembered for something equally powerful: investing in people. His ministry was marked by teaching, guidance, encouragement, and helping others grow. For fathers, Elisha represents the man who sees his role not merely as providing for his children but preparing them.

Core Strength: Development

Fatherhood Focus: Coaching, teaching, encouraging, and helping others reach their God-given potential.

Elisha Learned Before He Led

> *"Elisha son of Shaphat—left his oxen and ran after Elijah."* — **1 Kings 19:19-21**

Great mentors are first teachable. Before Elisha could develop others, he allowed himself to be developed.

Apply This To My Life

Who is currently mentoring or investing in my growth as a father?

What am I intentionally doing to keep growing and learning?

How Elisha Invested in Future Leaders

One of Elisha's greatest contributions was building a community of future prophets. Mentors multiply themselves. They don't seek followers; they develop leaders.

Apply This To My Life

What specific life skills, gifts, or lessons am I intentionally passing on to my children?

How Elisha Encouraged Growth

> *"Tell me, what do you have in your house?"* — **2 Kings 4:2**

Instead of immediately solving a widow's problem, Elisha helped her recognize resources she already possessed. Growth often happens through guided discovery.

Apply This To My Life

Instead of always giving answers, mentor fathers ask questions:

- "What do you think is the best solution?"
- "What have you learned from this?"
- "What gifts has God given you?"

Think of a recent situation where I gave an answer I could have turned into a question. What would that question have been?

How Elisha Developed Confidence

"Don't be afraid—Open his eyes, Lord, so that he may see." — **2 Kings 6:16-17**

When the prophet's servant panicked, Elisha responded with calm and prayer. A mentor father becomes a source of courage.

Apply This To My Life

What fear or insecurity in one of my children do I need to speak courage into?

How Elisha Left a Legacy

> *"Let me inherit a double portion of your spirit."* — **2 Kings 2:9**

The ultimate goal of mentoring is reproduction—you raise people who eventually help raise others. Successful fathers do not create dependence; they create capable adults.

Apply This To My Life

What legacy of mentorship am I building? How will my children invest in others because of what I modeled?

GO DEEPER

To go deeper on Love as the foundation of mentorship — and how to coach your children without controlling them — turn to the Love chapter in Fathering Strong: God's Blueprint for Leading Your Family.

A MENTOR IN REAL LIFE

James used to fix every problem his sons brought him — flat tires, fights with friends, homework. One evening he caught himself mid-answer and tried something different: "What do you think you should do?" His son hesitated, then answered his own question. James said nothing else. It was the quietest parenting win of his year — and the one that mattered most.

Strengths of the Mentor Father

- ✔ Enjoys teaching and encouraging growth
- ✔ Sees potential in others and invests in future generations
- ✔ Builds confidence
- ✔ Leads through influence rather than control

Blind Spots to Watch

- ⚠ Spending more time coaching than directing when direction is needed
- ⚠ Avoiding necessary discipline
- ⚠ Assuming growth will happen naturally without accountability

Mentoring works best when encouragement and standards work together.

Personal Reflection

Am I teaching my children or simply correcting them?

Do I see potential in my children that they cannot yet see in themselves?

How often do I ask questions instead of giving answers?

Who am I developing to become independent and capable?

My Action Plan: The Mentor

Based on what you've read, write one specific action you will take this week in each area:

One way I will apply this leadership style in my relationship with my children:

One conversation I need to have:

One habit or pattern I want to strengthen:

I will know I'm growing in this area when—

Fathering Strong Virtue: Love — a love that nurtures, develops, encourages, and calls others forward

Signed: ______________________________ *Date:* ____________

Chapter 4: Isaiah — The Visionary

Isaiah is perhaps the clearest example in Scripture of a visionary leader. While many prophets focused primarily on present problems, Isaiah continually pointed God's people toward what could be. For fathers, Isaiah represents the man who inspires his family with purpose, possibility, and God's bigger plan.

Core Strength: Vision

Fatherhood Focus: Inspiring purpose, hope, and future direction.

How Isaiah Saw Beyond Present Circumstances

> *"Forget the former things; do not dwell on the past. See, I am doing a new thing!"* — **Isaiah 43:18-19**

Isaiah ministered during political instability and fear. Yet he continually pointed people toward God's future. Visionaries help others see possibilities beyond current limitations.

Apply This To My Life

What present struggle in my family am I currently helping my children see with hope and perspective?

How Isaiah Inspired Purpose

> *"Here am I. Send me!"* — **Isaiah 6:8**

Visionaries help people connect their lives to a greater calling. A visionary father helps children discover not just what they do, but why they do it.

Apply This To My Life

How am I helping my children discover God's unique calling and gifts?

How Isaiah Cast a Picture of Hope

> *"Those who hope in the Lord will renew their strength. They will soar on wings like eagles."*
> **— Isaiah 40:31**

Isaiah didn't simply tell people to have faith. He gave them a compelling picture of what faith could produce. Vision creates motivation.

Apply This To My Life

What picture of the future am I painting for my children? Write out a few sentences of the vision you hold for each child:

How Isaiah Pointed Toward God's Bigger Story

> *"For to us a child is born, to us a son is given."* **— Isaiah 9:6**

Isaiah helped people understand that God was working toward redemption even when they couldn't see it. Visionaries help people trust God's plan before it becomes visible.

Apply This To My Life

How am I teaching my children that God is always working, even in difficult seasons?

How Isaiah Challenged People to Dream Bigger

> *"Enlarge the place of your tent."* **— Isaiah 54:2**

Visionaries challenge others to think beyond current limitations.

Apply This To My Life

What God-sized dream am I encouraging in my children?

How Isaiah Brought Comfort During Uncertainty

> *"Comfort, comfort my people, says your God."* — **Isaiah 40:1**

Vision without encouragement becomes pressure. Vision with encouragement becomes inspiration. Children need to hear: "You can do this. God is with you. Your future is bigger than this moment."

Apply This To My Life

What words of comfort and vision do I need to speak over my children right now?

GO DEEPER

To go deeper on Faith — and how to cast vision for your family without losing sight of the present — turn to the Faith chapter in Fathering Strong: God's Blueprint for Leading Your Family.

A VISIONARY IN REAL LIFE

After his daughter's third college rejection letter, Tom didn't pretend it didn't hurt. But that night he told her, "This isn't the whole story — it's one chapter." He reminded her of other closed doors that had turned out to be God redirecting her. She didn't feel better right away. But she remembered what he said, months later, when the right door finally opened.

Strengths of the Visionary Father

- ✔ Inspires others and thinks about the future
- ✔ Encourages big-picture thinking
- ✔ Casts compelling vision and builds hope
- ✔ Helps others discover purpose

Blind Spots to Watch

- ⚠ Focusing more on the future than the present moment
- ⚠ Becoming frustrated when others don't share the vision
- ⚠ Overlooking practical details

Visionaries often benefit from partnering with Builders who help turn vision into reality.

Personal Reflection

What vision do I have for my family?

Can my children clearly describe our family's purpose?

Do I regularly speak hope into my children's future?

What future possibilities do I see that my children cannot yet see?

My Action Plan: The Visionary

Based on what you've read, write one specific action you will take this week in each area:

One way I will apply this leadership style in my relationship with my children:

One conversation I need to have:

One habit or pattern I want to strengthen:

I will know I'm growing in this area when—

Fathering Strong Virtue: Faith — the ability to trust God's plan, see beyond present circumstances, and lead others toward a future not yet fully visible

Signed: ______________________________ *Date:* ____________

Chapter 5: Jeremiah — The Compassionate Shepherd

Known as the "Weeping Prophet," Jeremiah was unique because he not only delivered God's message—he felt the pain of the people he served. For fathers, Jeremiah represents the man who creates emotional safety, listens well, and develops deep relationships with those he loves.

Core Strength: Empathy

Fatherhood Focus: Building emotional connection, caring deeply for others, and walking alongside people through their struggles.

How Jeremiah Carried the Pain of Others

> *"Oh, that my head were a spring of water and my eyes a fountain of tears! I would weep day and night for the slain of my people."* — **Jeremiah 9:1**

Jeremiah didn't stand at a distance from people's struggles. Compassionate Shepherds feel with people, not just for people. Children often don't need immediate solutions—they need a father who understands.

A Compassionate Shepherd says "I understand" before saying "Here's what you should do."

Apply This To My Life

When was the last time I sat with one of my children through a disappointment without immediately trying to fix it?

How Jeremiah Listened to God's Heart

> *"I have loved you with an everlasting love."* — **Jeremiah 31:3**

Compassionate Shepherd fathers see beyond behavior. They ask: What is my child feeling? What is causing this reaction? What need is underneath this behavior?

Apply This To My Life

Think of a recent conflict or tension with one of your children. What might have been the underlying need or emotion driving their behavior?

How Jeremiah Created Emotional Connection

> *"My heart is broken within me."* — **Jeremiah 23:9**

Unlike many leaders who hide emotion, Jeremiah openly expressed his struggles. Authenticity creates connection. Children connect with fathers who are emotionally available.

Apply This To My Life

How comfortable am I expressing my own emotions to my children? What might I be modeling about emotional openness?

How Jeremiah Offered Hope During Pain

> *""For I know the plans I have for you," declares the Lord, "plans to prosper you and not to harm you, plans to give you hope and a future.""* — **Jeremiah 29:11**

This promise came during one of Israel's darkest seasons. Compassion does not ignore suffering—it walks through suffering while holding onto hope.

Apply This To My Life

Which of your children is currently in a painful or difficult season? What hope do you need to speak over them?

GO DEEPER

To go deeper on Love expressed through empathy and presence — turn to the Love chapter in Fathering Strong: God's Blueprint for Leading Your Family.

A COMPASSIONATE SHEPHERD IN REAL LIFE

When his son lost the championship game, Carlos's instinct was to break down everything that went wrong. Instead, he just sat next to him in the car, said "That stings," and let the silence do its work. Twenty minutes later, his son started talking on his own. Compassionate Shepherds know that being understood comes before being advised.

Strengths of the Compassionate Shepherd Father

- ✔ Listens deeply and creates emotional safety
- ✔ Empathizes without judgment
- ✔ Builds strong relational bonds
- ✔ Offers comfort and hope

Blind Spots to Watch

- ⚠ Avoiding necessary correction because conflict feels unkind
- ⚠ Enabling rather than empowering
- ⚠ Struggling to set firm boundaries

Compassion is strongest when paired with truth and healthy limits.

Personal Reflection

Do my children feel truly heard by me?

When do I tend to move too quickly from listening to advising?

How do I handle my own emotional pain, and what am I modeling to my children?

Am I creating a home where emotions are welcomed, not shut down?

My Action Plan: The Compassionate Shepherd

Based on what you've read, write one specific action you will take this week in each area:

One way I will apply this leadership style in my relationship with my children:

One conversation I need to have:

One habit or pattern I want to strengthen:

I will know I'm growing in this area when—

Fathering Strong Virtue: Love — a love that is emotionally present, empathetically available, and willing to enter into the suffering of others

Signed: ______________________________ *Date:* ____________

Chapter 6: Ezekiel — The Watchman

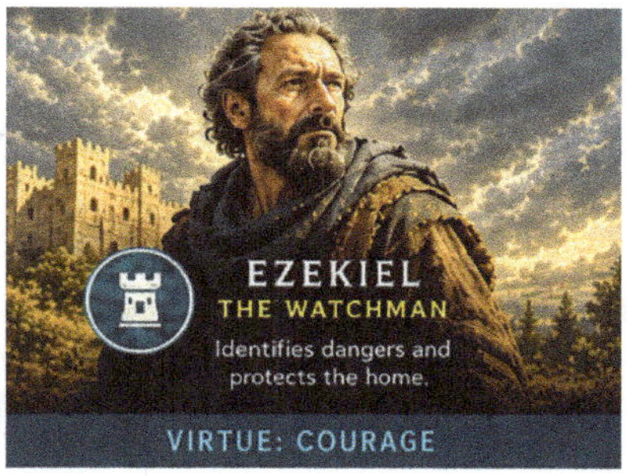

Ezekiel was called to be a watchman—someone who stood on the walls of the city, watched for danger, and warned the people. For fathers, Ezekiel represents the man who stays alert to dangers—spiritual, cultural, relational—and acts to protect and guide his family before crises develop.

Core Strength: Vigilance

Fatherhood Focus: Staying alert to threats, setting wise boundaries, and guiding the family with discernment.

The Watchman's Call

> *"Son of man, I have made you a watchman for the people of Israel; so hear the word I speak and give them warning from me."* — **Ezekiel 3:17**

Ezekiel was not called to control outcomes—he was called to be faithful in warning. Watchman fathers stay awake when others are asleep.

Apply This To My Life

What dangers—spiritual, relational, or cultural—do I sense approaching my family that I need to address?

How Ezekiel Stayed Faithful Despite Resistance

Ezekiel ministered to a people who largely rejected his message. Yet he remained faithful. Watchman fathers understand that faithfulness does not guarantee immediate results.

Apply This To My Life

Where am I faithfully holding a boundary or standard even when my children resist it?

How Ezekiel Discerned the Times

Watchmen see beneath the surface. They ask not just "What is happening?" but "Why is this happening?"

Apply This To My Life

What is one behavior or pattern in one of my children that I sense has a deeper root? What might God be showing me?

How Ezekiel Set Boundaries from Love

Ezekiel's warnings were not expressions of anger—they came from God's heart of love. Watchman fathers set boundaries not to control but to protect.

Apply This To My Life

Examine one boundary I have set in my home. Is it motivated more by love or by control?

Is there a boundary I need to establish that I have been avoiding?

GO DEEPER

To go deeper on Courage applied to discernment and protection — turn to the Courage chapter in Fathering Strong: God's Blueprint for Leading Your Family.

A WATCHMAN IN REAL LIFE

Weeks before anyone else noticed, Daniel sensed his son was drifting — quieter at dinner, more time alone in his room. He didn't wait for a crisis. He started showing up a little earlier to pick him up from practice, just for ten extra minutes in the car. No lecture — just availability. The Watchman's job isn't to predict the future. It's to pay attention to the present long enough to catch what others miss.

Strengths of the Watchman Father

- ✔ Stays alert to spiritual and cultural dangers
- ✔ Acts proactively rather than reactively
- ✔ Sets wise, loving boundaries
- ✔ Discerns what is happening beneath the surface
- ✔ Remains faithful even without immediate results

Blind Spots to Watch

- ⚠ Becoming overly suspicious or anxious
- ⚠ Turning protection into control
- ⚠ Carrying the weight of vigilance alone
- ⚠ Protecting out of fear rather than love

Personal Reflection

What warning signs am I seeing in my family that I haven't fully addressed?

Am I proactive in protecting my family or mostly reactive after problems arise?

Am I protecting out of fear or out of love?

Who else is standing watch with me? Am I doing this alone?

My Action Plan: The Watchman

Based on what you've read, write one specific action you will take this week in each area:

One way I will apply this leadership style in my relationship with my children:

One conversation I need to have:

One habit or pattern I want to strengthen:

I will know I'm growing in this area when—

Fathering Strong Virtue: Courage — the willingness to stay alert, speak difficult truths, and guard what God has entrusted to your care

Signed: ______________________________ *Date:* ____________

Chapter 7: Daniel — The Faithful Example

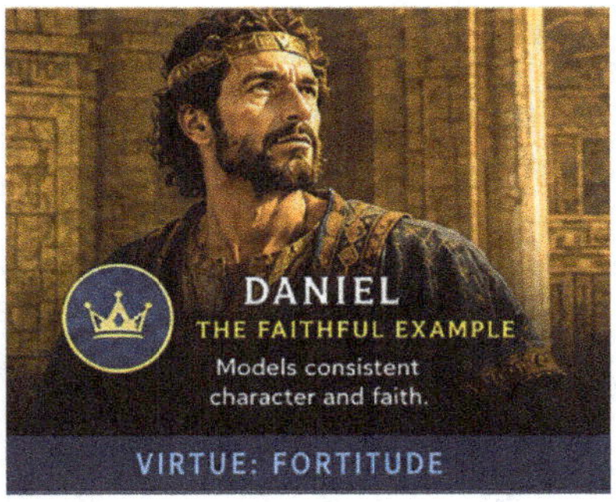

Daniel's life demonstrates one powerful truth: people are influenced more by what we consistently do than by what we occasionally say. For fathers, Daniel represents the man whose actions and faith create a model worth following.

Core Strength: Integrity

Fatherhood Focus: Modeling consistent character, unwavering faith, and godly leadership through personal example.

How Daniel Maintained Integrity in Difficult Environments

> *"Daniel resolved not to defile himself with the royal food and wine."* — **Daniel 1:8**

Character is often revealed in small decisions long before it is tested in major ones. Children watch how fathers respond to everyday choices: honesty, work ethic, commitments, relationships, personal discipline.

Apply This To My Life

In what small, everyday moments am I currently setting an example of integrity for my children?

Where am I tempted to compromise in ways my children might notice?

How Daniel Aligned His Actions With His Beliefs

> *"In every matter of wisdom and understanding—they found them ten times better."* **— Daniel 1:20**

Daniel did not separate faith from daily life. Children notice whether a father's actions match his words. The strongest influence comes from fathers who practice what they preach.

Apply This To My Life

Is there a gap between what I say I believe and how I actually live? Where is that gap most visible to my children?

How Daniel Remained Faithful Under Pressure

> *"When Daniel learned that the decree had been published, he went home—and prayed."* — **Daniel 6:10**

Daniel's enemies knew his faith was genuine and targeted it. He did not change his behavior to avoid consequences. Character remains steady when circumstances change.

Apply This To My LifeE

What recent difficult season tested my consistency? What did my children observe in how I responded?

How Daniel Earned Trust Through Consistency

> *"They could find no corruption in him, because he was trustworthy and neither corrupt nor negligent."* **— Daniel 6:4**

Trust is built through consistent behavior over time. Children thrive when they know what to expect from their father.

Apply This To My Life

Would my children describe me as dependable and consistent? What would they say?

How Daniel Demonstrated Courageous Humility

> *"There is a God in heaven who reveals mysteries."* — **Daniel 2:28**

Daniel possessed extraordinary gifts, yet consistently gave credit to God. True integrity includes humility.

Apply This To My Life

How am I modeling gratitude, humility, and dependence on God to my children?

GO DEEPER

To go deeper on Fortitude as it relates to consistency and integrity over the long haul — turn to the Fortitude chapter in Fathering Strong: God's Blueprint for Leading Your Family.

A FAITHFUL EXAMPLE IN REAL LIFE

Nobody was watching when Robert told his client the full truth about a mistake that would cost him the contract — except his son, half-asleep in the back seat, when Robert made the call from the car. He never mentioned it again. Years later, his son brought it up unprompted — it was the moment he decided what kind of businessman he wanted to be. Faithful Example fathers rarely know which moment their children are watching, so they stay consistent in all of them.

Strengths of the Faithful Example Father

- ✔ Lives with integrity and keeps commitments
- ✔ Demonstrates consistent faith and models godly character
- ✔ Remains dependable and earns trust over time
- ✔ Leads through example

Blind Spots to Watch

- ⚠ Being perceived as overly serious or rigid
- ⚠ Expecting others to have the same level of discipline
- ⚠ Neglecting vulnerability while emphasizing strength

The healthiest Daniels balance integrity with compassion.

Personal Reflection

Do my actions consistently match my beliefs?

What example am I setting when life becomes difficult?

Where am I tempted to compromise my values?

What legacy of character am I leaving behind?

My Action Plan: The Faithful Example

Based on what you've read, write one specific action you will take this week in each area:

One way I will apply this leadership style in my relationship with my children:

One conversation I need to have:

One habit or pattern I want to strengthen:

I will know I'm growing in this area when—

Fathering Strong Virtue: Fortitude — the strength to remain steady under pressure, maintain convictions through adversity, and build a legacy of character

Signed: ______________________________ *Date:* ____________

Chapter 8: Jonah — The Redeemed Learner

Jonah may seem like an unusual choice for a fatherhood leadership style because he is remembered more for his failures than his successes. Yet that is exactly why he belongs. Unlike Moses, Daniel, or Elijah, Jonah reminds us that spiritual growth is not about perfection. It is about allowing God to transform us through our mistakes.

Core Strength: Humility

Fatherhood Focus: Learning from mistakes, growing through failure, accepting correction, and demonstrating that God can redeem imperfect people.

How Jonah Responded Imperfectly to God's Calling

> *"But Jonah ran away from the Lord."* — **Jonah 1:3**

God gave Jonah a mission. Jonah fled in the opposite direction. The question is not "Will I make mistakes?" The question is "What will I do when I do?"

Apply This To My Life

What is an area of fatherhood where I have been running rather than leaning in?

How Jonah Faced the Consequences of His Choices

> *"I know that it is my fault that this great storm has come upon you."* — **Jonah 1:12**

Jonah stopped blaming others. He accepted responsibility. Growth begins when excuses end.

Apply This To My Life

Is there a situation in my home where I have blamed others instead of taking responsibility? What would it look like to own it?

How Jonah Learned in the Middle of Failure

> *"From inside the fish Jonah prayed to the Lord his God."* — **Jonah 2:1**

The fish was not merely a punishment. It became a classroom. Failure often becomes one of God's greatest teaching tools. Instead of asking "Why did this happen to me?" Redeemed Learners ask "What can God teach me through this?"

Apply This To My Life

What has a recent failure or setback taught me about myself as a father?

How Jonah Accepted a Second Chance

> *"Then the word of the Lord came to Jonah a second time."* — **Jonah 3:1**

God did not discard Jonah. God recommissioned him. Failure is an event, not a permanent label. Children need fathers who understand grace because they have experienced grace themselves.

Apply This To My Life

Where do I need to receive God's grace for a failure in my fathering? Write a prayer of honesty here:

How Jonah Grew Through Obedience

> *"Jonah obeyed the word of the Lord and went to Nineveh."* — **Jonah 3:3**

The second time, Jonah obeyed. His obedience led to one of the greatest revivals in Scripture. God can use imperfect people to accomplish extraordinary things.

Apply This To My Life

What is one area where God is calling me to obey, even though I've resisted or struggled with it?

The Power of Humility

Perhaps Jonah's greatest contribution is that his failures were preserved in Scripture. The book of Jonah contains his disobedience, his fear, his anger, his pride—yet God allowed those struggles to be recorded for future generations. People often learn more from our failures than our successes. Children benefit when fathers admit:

- *"I was wrong."*
- *"I need forgiveness."*
- *"I'm still learning."*
- *"Let's grow together."*

> *Humility builds trust. At its core, Jonah's story is not about failure. It is about redemption: "Salvation comes from the Lord." (Jonah 2:9)*

Apply This To My Life

How do I typically respond when I fail as a father? What would a more humble response look like?

GO DEEPER

To go deeper on Faith and what it means to trust God's grace after failure — turn to the Faith chapter in Fathering Strong: God's Blueprint for Leading Your Family.

A REDEEMED LEARNER IN REAL LIFE

After raising his voice at his daughter over something that, in hindsight, didn't deserve it, Anthony did something his own father never did: he knocked on her door, apologized specifically, and asked her to forgive him. She was twelve. She still remembers it as the moment she trusted him more, not less. Redeemed Learners understand that credibility isn't built by never failing — it's built by how honestly you respond when you do.

Strengths of the Redeemed Learner Father

- ✔ Admits mistakes and learns from failure
- ✔ Remains teachable and extends grace to others
- ✔ Demonstrates humility and embraces personal growth
- ✔ Understands God's forgiveness and passes it on

Blind Spots to Watch

- ⚠ Avoiding difficult responsibilities
- ⚠ Letting emotions control decisions
- ⚠ Becoming discouraged by failure
- ⚠ Repeating lessons that have not been fully learned

Growth requires intentional reflection and obedience.

Personal Reflection

How do I typically respond when I fail?

Do my children see me admit mistakes and ask for forgiveness?

What lessons has God taught me through hardship?

Am I creating a home where failure becomes a learning opportunity, not a source of shame?

My Action Plan: The Redeemed Learner

Based on what you've read, write one specific action you will take this week in each area:

One way I will apply this leadership style in my relationship with my children:

One conversation I need to have:

One habit or pattern I want to strengthen:

I will know I'm growing in this area when—

Fathering Strong Virtue: Faith — trusting that God remains faithful even when we stumble, and that He continually calls us forward

Signed: ______________________________ *Date:* ___________

Chapter 9: My Leadership Style Summary

Use this page to capture your key takeaways after working through all eight leadership styles.

Which leadership style felt most like me? Why?

Which leadership style challenged me or revealed an area I need to grow in?

What is the single most important thing this playbook surfaced about my fathering?

What does the father I want to become look like? Describe him:

My Fathering Strong Commitment

Write a personal commitment statement—a declaration of the kind of father you are choosing to become. Sign and date it.

Signed: ______________________________

Date: ________________________________

Chapter 10: Your Journey Continues

What You Do Next Is What Defines You

Completing this playbook is not the finish line. It is the starting block.

You have done the reflective work—you have identified your primary leadership style, faced your blind spots honestly, and committed to specific next steps in each chapter. That kind of self-awareness is rare. But self-awareness without continued action will fade. The goal now is to take what you have learned and build it into the daily fabric of your fatherhood.

The following resources were designed specifically to help you do that. Each one picks up where this playbook leaves off.

Your Next Steps

Resource 1: Fathering Strong—God's Blueprint For Leading Your Family

Real Stories with Biblical Wisdom to Guide your Fatherhood Journey. This is the primary reference companion to this playbook. It goes deep into the four core virtues—Courage, Fortitude, Faith, and Love—and the six foundational strengths that define intentional fatherhood. Through real stories, Scripture, and practical wisdom, it builds the framework that every chapter in this playbook draws from.

Available in print, Kindle, and Audible.

Resource 2: Fathering Strong—Fatherhood Awakening and 30-Day Devotional and Journal

Let your vision inspire you. Let your core virtues guide you. Let your SMART goals direct you. Let love motivate every step forward.

This companion resource takes the insights you developed in this playbook and turns them into a daily practice. The Fatherhood Awakening section helps you build a clear, written vision for the father you are becoming. The 30-Day Devotional and Journal gives you the daily structure to document your progress, reflect on your growth, and return again and again to who God is calling you to be.

Resource 3: Fathering Strong—A 90-Day Devotional Journey

Building the Father God Called You to Be with Courage, Fortitude, Faith and Love. Ninety days. Four virtues. One sustained commitment to becoming the father your family needs. This devotional is designed for the long haul—for the father who understands that meaningful change does not happen in a weekend but through steady, daily faithfulness over time.

Available in print, Kindle, and Audible.

A Final Word

> *"The goal is not perfection. The goal is intentional, growing, God-dependent fatherhood."*

Your children do not need a perfect father. They need a present one—a man who shows up, keeps growing, acknowledges when he gets it wrong, and never stops trying to become who God made him to be.

That father is who you are becoming. These eight prophets, with all of their strength and all of their failure, point the way.

Appendix A: Facilitator's Guide

The following section is for leaders using this playbook with a group of men.

Thank you for your willingness to facilitate this six-week journey through The Father You Were Made To Be. Leading other fathers through the assessment and the eight prophets is both a privilege and a responsibility. This guide will help you create an environment where men can be honest about the leaders they already are, the blind spots that come with their strengths, and the next step God is calling them to take.

This guide is designed to run alongside the playbook itself. It assumes every man in your group has his own copy, has completed (or will complete) the Fatherhood Leadership Style Assessment, and will read each chapter — including the Apply This to My Life prompts, Personal Reflection questions, and My Action Plan — before the session where it is discussed.

Your Role as Facilitator

You are not expected to be a perfect father, a licensed counselor, or an expert on all eight leadership styles. Your role is to:

- Create a safe space where men can be honest about their assessment results, their strengths, and their blind spots.
- Guide the discussion without dominating it — the eight prophets should do most of the teaching.
- Model vulnerability by naming your own Primary and Secondary Leadership Style, and a real blind spot, before you ask the group to.
- Keep the group focused on practical application to their own fatherhood, not abstract Bible trivia about Moses, Elijah, or the other prophets.
- Encourage accountability between sessions.
- Point men back to Scripture as the authority behind each leadership style, not to your own opinion or theirs.
- Pray for and with the men in your group, by name, throughout the six weeks.

Remember: this playbook is a mirror, not a test that men pass or fail. As the book itself puts it, these are "Eight Prophets. Many Flaws. One God." You are helping each man see, clearly and without shame, the father God has already begun shaping in him — and the next step he is being called to take. Your authenticity about your own leadership style will give other men permission to be real about theirs.

Preparing to Facilitate

Before the First Session

- Complete the assessment and read the entire playbook yourself first, including scoring your own results and filling out your own Assessment Summary, Visualize Your Results chart, Personal Reflection pages, and My Action Plan for each chapter. You cannot lead men where you have not gone yourself.

• Pray for each participant by name, asking God to prepare his heart and give him courage to be honest.

• Secure the logistics: a comfortable, private meeting space; a 90–120 minute time block for each session (weeks with two prophets will run toward the longer end); enough printed copies of the playbook, or make sure every man has his own; refreshments if possible.

• Set clear expectations up front: the six-week commitment, weekly attendance, reading the assigned chapter(s) and completing the Personal Reflection and My Action Plan sections before each session, and confidentiality.

Before Each Session

• Review the week's chapter(s) thoroughly. In Weeks 2–5 you are covering two prophets per session, so budget roughly twice the preparation time you would give a single chapter.

• Pray specifically for the session — for open hearts, honest discussion, and real transformation.

• Prepare your own story: a personal example tied to that week's leadership style(s) that you can share to model vulnerability.

• Arrive early. Set up the space, have materials ready, and be available to greet men as they arrive.

Weekly Session Format

Week 1 and Week 6 each focus on a single body of content (the assessment, and the wrap-up, respectively). Weeks 2–5 each cover two prophets, so the format below stretches to fit two teaching blocks instead of one. If a 100–120 minute block is not realistic for your group, an equally valid option is to split each of Weeks 2–5 into two shorter meetings, one prophet per meeting — simply double the number of sessions and keep everything else in this guide the same.

• Opening (10 minutes) — welcome, brief check-in, opening prayer, quick review of last week's My Action Plan commitment (after Week 1).

• First Prophet — Teaching and Discussion (30–40 minutes) — brief overview of the leadership style and its biblical foundation (5 minutes), group discussion of the chapter's Scripture and Apply This to My Life prompts (25–35 minutes), personal application sharing.

• Second Prophet — Teaching and Discussion (30–40 minutes) — same structure as above, applied to the week's second leadership style.

• Accountability and Application (15–20 minutes) — review of each man's Assessment Summary as it relates to this week's two styles, sharing from Personal Reflection and My Action Plan, pairing up for accountability.

• Closing (10 minutes) — prayer requests focused on fatherhood challenges, closing prayer, preview of next week's reading.

The Six-Week Schedule at a Glance

Week	Focus	Content Covered
1	Orientation & Assessment	How to Use Your Playbook; Why These Eight Prophets?; Eight Prophets. Many Flaws. One God.; The Fatherhood Leadership Style Assessment; My Assessment Summary; Visualize Your Results
2	Structure & Protection	Moses — The Builder; Elijah — The Courageous Protector
3	Development & Vision	Elisha — The Mentor; Isaiah — The Visionary
4	Compassion & Discernment	Jeremiah — The Compassionate Shepherd; Ezekiel — The Watchman
5	Integrity & Humility	Daniel — The Faithful Example; Jonah — The Redeemed Learner
6	Integration & Next Steps	My Leadership Style Summary; Quick Reference Guide; My Fathering Strong Commitment; Your Next Steps; A Final Word

Appendix B: Discussion Questions and Facilitator Notes for Each Week

Week 1: Orientation and the Assessment

Primary Goal

Introduce the framework of the eight prophets, walk every man through the assessment, and help each man record his Primary and Secondary Leadership Style and his Growth Opportunity in My Assessment Summary.

Key Emphasis

This is not a personality test and there are no bad scores. Every style in this playbook is a legitimate, biblical way to lead a family. The goal of tonight is self-awareness, not self-judgment.

Opening Question

"What leadership style do you think your own father had? How did that shape the father you've become?"

Walking Through The Assessment

Give the group 20–25 minutes of quiet, individual time to complete all 40 statements and score their eight totals — or, better, ask men to complete the assessment before arriving so the full session can be spent on discussion. Either way, build in time to:

• Walk through the 1–5 scoring scale together before anyone begins, so no one is guessing at what "Agree" versus "Strongly Agree" means.

• Have each man total his eight scores and transfer them to My Assessment Summary.

• Have each man shade in the Visualize Your Results chart and circle his Primary and Secondary Leadership Style rows.

• Have each man draw a line at his lowest score — that is this season's Growth Opportunity, not a permanent verdict.

Key Discussion Questions

1. Which leadership style scored highest for you? Does that surprise you, or does it confirm what you already suspected?

2. Which style scored lowest? How do you feel about that being named a "growth opportunity" rather than a weakness?

3. Think of a specific moment this week you led — or failed to lead — your children. Which of the eight leadership styles would have served that moment best?

4. Re-read "Eight Prophets. Many Flaws. One God." Which of the eight prophets' failures do you relate to most right now?

5. What are you hoping to walk away with after six weeks in this group?

Facilitator Tip

Scoring 40 statements and filling out the summary takes real time — build it into the 90–120 minute block, or send the assessment out ahead of time so men arrive with it already scored, leaving the full session for discussion and connection.

Watch For

Men who resist the categories ("I don't fit in a box"). Remind them the framework is descriptive, not restrictive — most fathers carry real strength in two or three styles. Also watch for men who are new to the group and feel exposed sharing their scores out loud; normalize a wide range of results and make clear that no score is shameful.

Application Focus

Each man commits to naming his Primary and Secondary Leadership Style and his one Growth Opportunity out loud before he leaves tonight.

Week 2: The Builder (Moses) & The Courageous Protector (Elijah)

Primary Goal

Help men recognize the concrete, specific ways they already provide structure and protection for their families — and see where those same strengths tip into rigidity or control.

Key Emphasis

Structure and protection are often the two things men were taught fatherhood is only about ("provide and defend"). Tonight is not about proving they already do these things. It is about precision: naming specifically how they build, specifically how they protect, and where each strength has a shadow side.

Opening Question

"Which of these two men — Moses or Elijah — sounds more like the father you had growing up? Which sounds more like the father you are now?"

The Builder — Moses

Key Discussion Questions

1. Read Exodus 18:21 together. What "capable men" — routines, systems, or people — have you put in place so you're not the only thing holding your household together?

2. What values would your kids say your family stands for — not what you'd say, what they'd say?

3. Where has structure become more important to you than the relationship it's supposed to protect?

4. Moses kept leading even after Israel's worst failure, the golden calf. Where have you wanted to walk away instead of staying and rebuilding?

Facilitator Tip

This chapter tends to produce two extremes — men proud of the systems they've built, and men who feel like they have no systems and feel behind. Both reactions are useful; don't let either one dominate the room.

Watch For

Men whose "structure" has become control — inflexible schedules, rigid rules with no room for a child's individuality, or an inability to rest. The chapter's own Blind Spots to Watch list names this directly; use it.

The Courageous Protector — Elijah

Key Discussion Questions

1. Read 1 Kings 18:21. Where in your family's life right now do you need to stop "wavering between two opinions" and take a clear stand?

2. Elijah's protection included the practical (flour and oil for the widow) as well as the confrontational (facing Ahab). Which kind of protecting comes more naturally to you — practical provision or direct confrontation?

3. Elijah collapsed into despair and isolation right after his greatest victory (1 Kings 19). Where do you tend to crash after a hard season of holding everything together?

4. Who protects you? Who do you let see you when you're the one who's afraid?

Facilitator Tip

Many men will describe protection only in terms of physical safety or finances. Push gently toward the harder category — protecting a child's heart, faith, and self-worth from harmful words, relationships, or influences.

Watch For

Men using "protection" language to justify controlling or domineering behavior toward their wife or children. If this surfaces, address it directly and privately after the session — see "When to Refer Out."

Application Focus

Each man identifies one system he needs to build (Moses) and one thing he needs to stand up and protect (Elijah) this week — and names both out loud before the group.

Week 3: The Mentor (Elisha) & The Visionary (Isaiah)

Primary Goal

Help men move from providing and protecting toward developing others and casting vision — the more relational, future-facing leadership styles.

Key Emphasis

Building and protecting are about the present and the perimeter. Mentoring and vision-casting are about someone else's future. This is often a harder shift for task-oriented men — from "what do I need to do" to "who am I developing, and toward what?"

Opening Question

"Who mentored you — as a man, in your faith, in your work? What did they do that made the difference?"

The Mentor — Elisha

Key Discussion Questions

1. Elisha asked for "a double portion" of Elijah's spirit — he wanted more responsibility, not less. Are you actively pursuing your own growth right now, or coasting?

2. Read 2 Kings 4:2. Elisha started with what the widow already had. What gift or interest does each of your children already have that you could build on this week, instead of pushing your own agenda?

3. Where are you doing things for your children that you should be teaching them to do for themselves?

4. What competes for your undivided attention with your kids, and what would it cost to shut that door?

Facilitator Tip

This chapter often surfaces guilt around distraction — phones, work, exhaustion. Normalize the struggle, then move quickly to one concrete change rather than dwelling in guilt.

Watch For

Men who mentor everyone except their own children — coaching a team, discipling other men, but not investing the same energy at home. Name the pattern gently, without shaming.

The Visionary — Isaiah

Key Discussion Questions

1. Isaiah could see what was coming when no one else could. What "former things" — old failures, an old label, an old family pattern — are you still letting define one of your children?

2. Isaiah's answer to God's call was immediate: "Here am I. Send me!" What is God currently asking of you as a father that you've been slow to say yes to?

3. Have you ever told your children, in specific words, what you believe God's purpose is for your family? If not, what's stopped you?

4. Visionary fathers can leave people inspired but unsupported. Where do you cast vision for your family without following through on the practical steps to get there?

Facilitator Tip

Isaiah's chapter can feel abstract next to Elisha's very practical one. Keep bringing the group back to one specific sentence each man could say to one specific child this week.

Watch For

Men who use "vision" language to avoid present responsibilities — always talking about the future instead of doing today's work. Pair this chapter's challenge with last week's Builder chapter as a check.

Application Focus

Each man names one child he will intentionally develop (Elisha) and one specific, hope-filled word he will speak about the family's future (Isaiah) before the next session.

Week 4: The Compassionate Shepherd (Jeremiah) & The Watchman (Ezekiel)

Primary Goal

Help men hold two strengths in tension that are often seen as opposites — deep emotional presence (Jeremiah) and clear-eyed discernment of danger (Ezekiel) — and see that a father needs both.

Key Emphasis

Many men were taught that being emotionally available and being vigilant or protective are in conflict — that you're either the "soft" parent or the "strict" one. Jeremiah and Ezekiel show these are not opposites; they are both forms of love.

Opening Question

"Growing up, was your home more of a place where feelings were welcome, or a place where problems were solved? What did that teach you?"

The Compassionate Shepherd — Jeremiah

Key Discussion Questions

1. Jeremiah carried the pain of the people he served as his own. When was the last time you let one of your children's pain actually affect you, instead of moving straight to fixing it?

2. Jeremiah kept showing up despite rejection and mockery. Where has a relationship with one of your children gone quiet, and what would it look like to keep showing up anyway?

3. Do your children know they can cry, fail, or fall apart in front of you without you flinching or fixing?

4. Where do you need to set a boundary so that carrying your family's emotional weight doesn't burn you out?

Facilitator Tip

This chapter can be the most vulnerable one in the whole playbook. Slow down. Don't rush to the next question if a man is visibly moved.

Watch For

Men who are emotionally flooded — absorbing everyone's pain with no outlet of their own. Ask directly who they process with, and encourage a counselor or pastor if they have no one.

The Watchman — Ezekiel

Key Discussion Questions

1. Read Ezekiel 3:17. What's one influence — a friendship, an app, a habit, a cultural message — you can see approaching your family that you haven't named out loud yet?
2. Ezekiel set boundaries from love, not fear. How would your kids describe your warnings — protective, or controlling?
3. What does the spiritual climate of your home look like right now — is prayer, Scripture, and worship rare or regular?
4. Where have you stayed silent when you knew you should have spoken up?

Facilitator Tip

Watchman fathers often over-index on threats. Balance every "watch for" question with a "what's going right" question so the conversation doesn't become fear-driven.

Watch For

Men whose discernment has curdled into anxiety or control — suspicion of every friendship, every screen, every outside influence. This chapter's own Blind Spots to Watch list names this directly; use it.

Application Focus

Each man names one child he will sit with emotionally, without fixing (Jeremiah), and one specific influence he will address as watchman this week (Ezekiel).

Week 5: The Faithful Example (Daniel) & The Redeemed Learner (Jonah)

Primary Goal

Close the individual-chapter portion of the playbook with the two "character" styles — the consistency of Daniel and the humility of Jonah — setting up next week's integration.

Key Emphasis

Daniel and Jonah are often seen as opposites — the man who never fails, and the man who fails loudly — but both chapters teach the same thing: what matters is what a man does with pressure and with failure, not whether he is ever perfect.

Opening Question

"Where in your life right now does the private version of you and the public version of you look most different?"

The Faithful Example — Daniel

Key Discussion Questions

1. Daniel maintained integrity in a culture designed to reshape his identity. What's a small, unglamorous line you've drawn that your kids may not even notice, but that keeps your integrity intact?

2. Daniel prayed "just as he had done before," even under threat of death. What's one discipline in your life that you keep even when no one's watching or when it costs you?

3. Is there a gap right now between what you say you believe and how you actually live? Name it, even just to yourself.

4. Faithful Example fathers can become rigid or hard to approach. Do your kids feel free to come to you with failure, or do they feel judged?

Facilitator Tip

Some men will hear "consistency" as "perfection" and shut down. Clarify early: Daniel's strength was faithfulness under pressure, not flawlessness.

Watch For

Men holding themselves — or their kids — to standards that leave no room for grace: perfectionism dressed up as integrity.

The Redeemed Learner — Jonah

Key Discussion Questions

1. Jonah ran, failed spectacularly, and hit rock bottom before he learned. What "belly of the fish" season taught you the most about yourself as a father — and are you still resisting a lesson from it?

2. Do your kids ever see you admit you were wrong — out loud, without excuse?

3. Jonah was still angry and resentful even after Nineveh repented. What unresolved resentment or pride are you still carrying that your family can probably sense?

4. What would it look like to tell one of your kids a real story of your own failure and what God did with it?

Facilitator Tip

This is a natural moment for you as facilitator to model vulnerability first — share a specific failure and what you learned from it, before asking the group to do the same.

Watch For

Men stuck at either extreme — false humility that never moves past self-flagellation, or defensiveness that can't admit fault at all. Both need the same next step: naming one specific thing and one specific repair.

Application Focus

Each man names one place he needs Daniel's consistency and one place he needs Jonah's humility — and shares one story of failure and growth with the group or an accountability partner.

Week 6: The Integrated Father — Wrap-Up and Next Steps

Primary Goal

Help each man see his eight scores as one integrated picture instead of eight separate boxes, complete My Fathering Strong Commitment, celebrate six weeks of growth, and leave with a specific 90-day plan using Your Next Steps.

Key Emphasis

The goal was never to make every man a Builder, or an Elisha. The goal is integration: using a primary style as a strength, a secondary style for range, and treating the lowest score as this season's growth assignment — not a permanent grade.

Opening Question

"Of everything from the last five weeks, what's the one moment or verse that has stuck with you?"

Facilitator Notes for the Final Session

- Review the Quick Reference Guide: The Eight Leadership Styles at a Glance together.
- Have each man restate his Primary and Secondary Leadership Style and his Growth Opportunity from Week 1 — has anything shifted after five weeks of reflection?
- Give time for each man to complete My Fathering Strong Commitment — a signed, dated personal declaration — either in the session or as that week's take-home step.
- Celebrate growth: go around the circle and have each man share one way he's grown as a father, one specific change he's made, and one thing he's grateful for.
- Walk through Your Next Steps together — the resources designed to help the group keep growing after this playbook ends.
- Close by having each man pray for the man on his right, specifically for his growth as a father.

Key Discussion Questions

1. Has your Primary or Secondary Leadership Style shifted at all now that you've studied all eight — or been confirmed?
2. Which of the other seven fathers challenged you the most this study, and why?
3. What is one specific, 90-day goal tied to your lowest-scoring leadership style?

4. How do you want this group to continue — keep meeting, study another Fathering Strong resource together, or send some of you out to start new groups?

Facilitator Tip

Resist the urge to rush this session. Six weeks of honest work deserves an unhurried closing — protect the full 90–120 minutes and don't sacrifice the celebration and prayer time for one more discussion question.

Watch For

Men who want to end quietly without naming a specific next step. A vague "I'll keep working on it" rarely survives contact with real life — press gently for one concrete, dated commitment before they leave, ideally written into My Fathering Strong Commitment.

Action Item

Every man leaves with his Primary/Secondary Leadership Style and Growth Opportunity written down, a signed My Fathering Strong Commitment, one 90-day goal, and a decision about how the group will continue.

Facilitating Effective Discussions

Creating a Safe Environment

• Establish ground rules on the first night: what's shared in the group stays in the group; no fixing, advising, or correcting unless asked; everyone participates, but no one dominates; it's okay to pass if you're not ready to share; every leadership style and parenting approach in the room is respected; focus on your own growth, not on judging another man's style or family.

• Model vulnerability first. Share your own Primary and Secondary Leadership Style, a real Blind Spot to Watch, and a real story before you ask the group to.

• Protect the space. Thank a man for his courage when he shares something personal. If someone dominates, redirect gently: "Thanks for that — let's hear from someone else."

• Avoid the fix-it trap. Especially with Builder- and Watchman-leaning men in the room, resist letting the group turn into problem-solving. Sometimes a man just needs to be heard.

Handling Difficult Situations

WHEN SOMEONE DOMINATES THE DISCUSSION

• "Thanks for that insight. Let's hear from someone who hasn't shared yet."

• Establish a "one share per question" norm if needed.

WHEN THE GROUP GETS OFF-TOPIC

• "That's an interesting point, but let's come back to the question at hand."

• "We could talk about that for hours, but let's stay focused on tonight's prophets."

WHEN SOMEONE PUSHES BACK ON HIS ASSESSMENT RESULTS

("I don't think that's really me" or "these labels feel like a personality test"): Remind the group this is a mirror, not a verdict. Invite the man to sit with a result for a week rather than argue it in the moment — sometimes the style we resist naming is the one closest to true.

WHEN SOMEONE SHARES SOMETHING CONCERNING

- (abuse, addiction, severe marital problems): Thank him for his honesty.
- Offer to talk with him privately after the session.
- Connect him with an appropriate resource — pastor, licensed counselor, or recovery program.
- Don't try to solve serious problems in the group setting. See "When to Refer Out" below.

WHEN THERE'S AWKWARD SILENCE

- Don't rush to fill it. Give men time to think.
- Rephrase the question if needed.
- Share your own answer first to get things started.

WHEN SOMEONE IS CLEARLY NOT DOING THE WORK BETWEEN SESSIONS

- Address it privately, not in the group.
- Ask if there are obstacles you can help remove.
- Remind him he'll get out of this what he puts into it.
- If it continues, have a direct conversation about his commitment to the group.

Using the Playbook's Reflection Tools

During the Session

- Don't just ask "did you finish the reflection questions?" Ask specific questions instead: "What score surprised you?" "What's one answer from your Personal Reflection or My Action Plan that you're willing to read out loud?"

- Have men share directly from their playbooks — a specific verse, a specific Apply This to My Life answer, a specific Strength or Blind Spot to Watch they recognized in themselves.

- Use each man's Assessment Summary and Visualize Your Results chart as an ongoing reference point each week: "This week's two prophets — where do they fall on your chart?"

Between Sessions

- Send a mid-week text or email pointing back to that week's My Action Plan commitment.
- Check in privately with men who seem to be falling behind.
- Celebrate progress publicly (with permission) at the start of the next session.

Building Accountability

Accountability Partners

• Pair men up in Week 1 or 2, once everyone has a completed Assessment Summary in hand. Consider pairing complementary styles — a Builder with a Shepherd, a Watchman with a Mentor — so partners can learn from each other's strength.

• Have partners exchange phone numbers and commit to a weekly check-in.

• Give them specific questions to ask each other: "Did you complete your My Action Plan step this week?" "Which leadership style did you lean on with your kids this week?" "Where did you struggle?" "How can I pray for you?"

Group Accountability

• Start each session (after Week 1) with a brief check-in on last week's My Action Plan commitment.

• Celebrate wins publicly. Create a culture where admitting failure is safe.

• Remind men that accountability is support, not shame.

Long-Term Accountability

• Encourage the group to keep meeting after Week 6.

• Suggest a next resource together from Your Next Steps — Fathering Strong: God's Blueprint for Leading Your Family, Fatherhood Awakening and 30-Day Devotional and Journal, or Fathering Strong: A 90-Day Devotional Journey.

• Help them build an ongoing rhythm of connection and accountability.

Prayer in the Group

Opening Prayer

• Keep it brief — one to two minutes.

• Ask God to open hearts, guide the discussion, and bring real transformation.

• Invite a different man to pray each week.

Closing Prayer

• Allow time for specific prayer requests related to fatherhood.

• Write down requests so you can follow up during the week.

• Pray specifically for each man's children, by name.

Between Sessions

• Pray for each man and his family during the week.

• Send encouraging texts letting men know you're praying for them.

• Keep a running group prayer list that you update weekly.

Final Session Checklist

In your Week 6 session, be sure you have:

• Celebrated growth — one way each man has grown, one specific change he's made, one thing he's grateful for.

• Reviewed the eight leadership styles using the Quick Reference Guide and each man's Primary, Secondary, and Growth Opportunity.

• Given time for My Fathering Strong Commitment to be written, signed, and dated.

• Helped each man choose one specific, 90-day growth goal.

• Reviewed Your Next Steps together and decided how the group will continue.

• Prayed for one another by name.

Continuing the Journey

• Keep meeting monthly for fellowship, accountability, and prayer.

• Work through one of the resources listed in Your Next Steps together as a group.

• Start a new group — have some of the men from your group facilitate new groups of their own, multiplying the impact.

• Create a dads' network — organize occasional events for fathers and children: service projects, camping trips, sports outings.

When to Refer Out

As a facilitator, you are not a professional counselor. Know when to point a man toward additional help:

• Abuse (past or present): if a man discloses that he is abusing his children or was abused as a child, connect him with a pastor or professional counselor.

• Addiction: if a man is struggling with addiction — alcohol, drugs, pornography, or otherwise — connect him with a recovery program or counselor.

• Severe marital problems: if a man's marriage is in crisis, encourage him to seek marriage counseling.

• Mental health issues: if a man is dealing with depression, anxiety, or any other mental health concern — including any mention of self-harm — take it seriously and connect him with a doctor or counselor right away. Do not try to handle it alone as a facilitator.

Your role is to provide support and point men toward appropriate resources, not to solve serious problems yourself.

Resources for Facilitators

Recommended Reading

All titles below are listed in this playbook's own Your Next Steps section:

- ***Fathering Strong — God's Blueprint for Leading Your Family,*** by Bruce Stapleton
- ***Fathering Strong: Fatherhood Awakening and 30-Day Devotional and Journal***, by Bruce Stapleton
- ***Fathering Strong — A 90-Day Devotional Journey,*** by Bruce Stapleton

Online Resources

- FatheringStrongBook.com — additional resourfces and the Fathering Strong email list (see Stay Connected).
- information@fatheringstrongbook.com — for bundle discounts on group materials for churches.

Final Encouragement

Leading this group is a significant investment of your time and energy. There will be moments when you wonder if it's making a difference. Trust that it is.

Every man who shows up and takes the assessment honestly is taking a courageous step. Every Personal Reflection answered without dodging is planting a seed. Every My Action Plan written down in faith is an act of trust. God is at work in ways you cannot see.

You are not just facilitating a workshop — you are helping shape the next generation. The impact of these six weeks will ripple out through the lives of these men, their children, their grandchildren, and beyond.

Thank you for your faithfulness. May God bless you and give you wisdom as you lead.

> *"Be strong and courageous. Do not be afraid; do not be discouraged, for the LORD your God will be with you wherever you go." (Joshua 1:9)*

About the Author

Bruce Stapleton is the author of the Fathering Strong series, including Fathering Strong: God's Blueprint for Leading Your Family, Fatherhood Awakening and 30-Day Devotional and Journal, and Fathering Strong: A 90-Day Devotional Journey. He combines over 25 years of teaching Christian adult education in parenting with hands-on leadership of fatherhood initiatives through Urban Light Ministries, where he serves as a Fathering Strong program leader and former Board Chairman alongside founder Pastor Eli Williams.

Bruce's background spans the corporate world and church ministries alike — from executive leadership at NCR Corporation, to creating the award-winning Lifegevity wellness program, to teaching college-level digital marketing. But his deepest credentials come from home: he is a father of four and grandfather of four, married 44 years, and a man still learning from what his own father and grandfather modeled for him about steady, faithful presence.

Bruce writes from the conviction that fatherhood is not a role to perform but a calling to grow into — one honest, Spirit-led step at a time.

Learn more or connect with Bruce at www.fatheringstrongbook.com.

MORE RESOURCES FROM FATHERING STRONG

Continue the journey with the full Fathering Strong resource library.

Fathering Strong: God's Blueprint for Leading Your Family

The foundational book in the Fathering Strong series. Combining more than 35 personal stories from the author's own journey raising four children with 85 real-world examples from 20 contributing fathers and 160+ biblical references, this book gives fathers practical wisdom built around four core virtues — courage, fortitude, faith, and love. Each chapter includes SMART goals, action steps, and prayer points to help fathers move from inspiration to daily implementation. Available in print, Kindle, and audiobook.

Fathering Strong: A 90-Day Devotional Journey

Building the Father God Called You to Be. A three-month devotional journey that helps fathers build lasting habits of courage, fortitude, faith, and love — one focused scripture and reflection at a time, in less than two minutes a day. A natural next step after reading Fathering Strong, this devotional turns the book's principles into daily practice. Available in print, digital, and audio.

Fathering Strong: Fatherhood Awakening and 30-Day Devotional and Journal

A 7-day awakening paired with a 30-day devotional journal that helps fathers write a personal Fatherhood Vision Statement, set SMART goals, and build the daily habits that turn intention into action. Designed as the ideal starting point for any man beginning his fatherhood journey, or as a companion resource for small groups and church workshops. Available in print.

A Father's Heart: A Bible Study Through Proverbs

A six-week Bible study that walks fathers through the book of Proverbs, applying its timeless wisdom to the everyday work of raising children. Each session pairs biblical teaching with reflection questions and practical action steps for raising wise, faithful children. Ideal for individual study, men's small groups, or as a deeper follow-up study after a Fathering Strong workshop. Available in print.

Church Workshop: Participant Workbook & Facilitator's Guide

Built for men's ministries, small groups, and weekend retreats, this companion set equips a church to run the full 12-week Fathering Strong workshop. The Facilitator's Guide gives leaders everything needed to run effective sessions, including session outlines, discussion prompts, and timing guides. The Participant Workbook leads each man through discussion questions and personal reflection exercises tied to video teaching sessions led by the author. Paired with the core book and session videos, these guides form a complete curriculum for building stronger fathers — and stronger churches.

Workshop kits are available for churches and ministry leaders, including bulk pricing for groups.

Learn more and order: fatheringstrongbook.com

www.ingramcontent.com/pod-product-compliance
Lightning Source LLC
LaVergne TN
LVHW061822080726
842811LV00007B/28